Eliot's *Objective Correlative*
Tradition or Individual Talent

T0355740

Eliot's *Objective Correlative*
Tradition or Individual Talent

Contributions to the History of a *Topos*

FLEMMING OLSEN

sussex
ACADEMIC
PRESS
Brighton • Chicago • Toronto

2 4 6 8 10 9 7 5 3 1

First published 2012 in Great Britain in the United Kingdom by
SUSSEX ACADEMIC PRESS
PO Box 139   Eastbourne BN24 9BP

Distributed in North America by
SUSSEX ACADEMIC PRESS
Independent Publishers Group
814 N. Franklin Street, Chicago, IL 60610

British Library Cataloguing in Publication Data
A CIP catalogue record for this book is available from the British Library.

Library of Congress Cataloguing-in-Publication Data
Olsen, Flemming.
Eliot's objective correlative : tradition or individual talent? :   contributions to the history of a topos / by Flemming Olsen.
p. cm.
Includes bibliographical references and index.
ISBN 978-1-84519-554-0 (p/b : acid-free paper)
1. Eliot, T. S. (Thomas Stearns), 1888–1965—Criticism and interpretation.
I. Title.
PS3509.L43Z7966 2012
821'.912—dc23

2012015909

Typeset by Sussex Academic Press, Brighton & Eastbourne.
Printed and bound by CPI Group (UK) Ltd, Croydon, CR0 4YY

CONTENTS

NOTE TO THE READER

French quotations running to more that a couple of words are given in their original formulation in the Notes. The English version that appears in the text is my own translation.

Il y a dans le mot, dans le *verbe,* quelque chose de *sacré,* qui nous défend d'en faire un jeu de hazard.

CHARLES BAUDELAIRE

INTRODUCTION

The only way of expressing emotion in the form of art is by finding an "objective correlative":

> in other words, a set of objects, a situation, a chain of events which shall be the formula of that *particular* emotion such that when the external facts, which must terminate in sensory experience, are given, the emotion is immediately evoked.

Is Eliot's "objective correlative" just an idiosyncratic rephrasing of the conventional formulation "the right word in the right place"? If so, critical reverence for the dictum is inversely proportional to its significance. Or is it a ground-breaking contribution to the centuries-old discussion of the relationship between *sensus* and *verbum*? In either case, Eliot's statement is intriguing and deserving of closer analysis. Obviously, any human communication is dependent on the participants' — the sender's and the receiver's — choice of words. A poet is a person who is endowed with a well-developed ear for words, and since he or she finds himself or herself in a specific communication situation — usually, there is no immediate response from a receiver — the demands on his or her control of the vocabulary are especially great.

Literary critics from Antiquity and onwards have dealt, more or less explicitly, with the capacity of language to describe what is conventionally called reality, to account for a person's feelings or the workings of his or her mind, or to characterize another human being or a situation.

However, Eliot does not give any sources or investigate any origins for his statement, which is remarkable, not only in the light of his awe-inspiring erudition and the effortless roaming in, and familiarity with, European literature that he demonstrates in his essays, but also when we consider his immense preoccupation with the use of words, their notional content, and their rhythmical sound.

Eliot, whom Hugh Kenner called "the most influential man of letters of the twentieth century"[1] never wrote, and never intended to write, an *ars poetica*. His critical output is to be found in the numerous critical essays he wrote on the oeuvres of mainly English and American, but to some extent also foreign authors' works — even though it must be admitted that some of his titles seem to promise more of an in-depth treatment than is actually offered.

Most of those essays date form the 1920s and 1930s, and in remarks scattered in his later writings, Eliot was at pains to emphasize that his taste within criticism changed with the increasing amount of literature that he read, and his growing life experience. The attitude is a faint echo of what his teacher, the philosopher Francis Herbert Bradley, once said: "The usual self of one period is not the usual self of another."[2] However, the dictum about the "objective correlative", which occurred originally in the *Hamlet* essay from 1920, was incorporated unaltered in the collection of essays *The Sacred Wood*, which appeared in 1928, and was preserved in the 1969 edition of that book. Eliot's preoccupation with the verbalization aspect also appears from the fact that even in essays dealing with philosophical or theological aspects he devotes a considerable amount of attention to the formulations chosen by the author of the analysed work.

The idea of the objective correlative is another illustration of Eliot's concern with the precise rendering of a poet's reactions. It is, on the one hand, an implicit warning against the vague effusions to be found in the feeble works of the Georgian poets who dominated the scene. On the other hand, it is a contribution to the old debate about poetic diction and about the relationship between language and reality. Eliot's emphasis on the verbal aspect, and, more generally, on form, fits in nicely with concerns prevalent in the literary climate and the intellectual Zeitgeist in the first two decades of the 20th century, when a reaction against what was felt as the dry rigidity of the Positivist world picture gathered momentum. The wording of the passage in which the objective correlative is presented is reminiscent of a Positivist axiomatic statement on a point of science: it is a fact that. . . .

The point is precision, not emotionalism: *objectivity* should be the sought-for ideal, and of course there is a *correlative*, a correspondence, which does not necessarily mean a one-to-one accord, between a writer's reaction to a stimulus from his surroundings and some item or phenomenon in those surroundings. The crux of the matter is to become aware of it and to express it adequately. The poet is not specifically referred to, but Eliot's formulation leaves us in no doubt that his words are meant as advice to, or even demands on, the poet, and such demands are not up for discussion.

As in Positivist science, the truth was not only obtainable, but also one and indivisible. However, as will appear in the following pages, Eliot's objective correlative raises at least as many hares as it shoots.

This book is not a systematic review of the ideas held by critics from Antiquity and onwards on the subject of the relationship between language and reality. Such a treatment would require volumes; hence the concentration has been on authors and critics who can be said, in some sense, to anticipate Eliot's theory.

CHAPTER ONE

SOME CLASSICAL PREDECESSORS

Aristotle

In the opening lines to the Introduction to his *Poetics*, Aristotle announces that "my design is to treat of poetry in general, and of its several species".[1] The "species" are categorized in the next paragraph: "epic poetry, tragedy, comedy, dithyrambics, as also, for the most part, the music of the flute and the lyre".[2]

Aristotle immediately proceeds to establish their common feature: they are all imitations of the actions of men. And what the Stagirite understands by 'imitation' is explained later in the *Poetics*:

> (The poet) "must represent things such as they were or are; or such as they are said to be and believed to be; or such as they should be, . . ."[3]

So, Aristotle assumes that there is such a thing as a world separate form the poet. For the concept of imitation to be at all meaningful, there must be something or somebody to imitate. Equally, he presupposes the existence of one or more recipients of the poet's achievement. Already in this very early theory, we meet the triad that has become a classic in communication theory, viz.

sender, message, and receiver. And Aristotle generalizes on behalf of mankind: "All men . . . naturally receive pleasure from imitation."[4] It is postulated that it is in man's *nature* to have a positive attitude to imitation.

Aristotle is himself an adherent of imitation: in viewing the works of art, "we contemplate with pleasure, and with the more pleasure the more they are imitated".[5] In his opinion, even rhythm, melody, and verse are "means of imitation".[6] Since words play a central part where imitation is concerned, they feature prominently in *Poetics* right from the beginning: "Words have a capacity to imitate",[7] and "the *epopeia* imitates by words alone, or by verse".[8] Eliot's theory is, *mutatis mutandis*, an echo of the former of those statements.

References to words, their composition and use occur regularly in *Poetics*. A noun is "a sound composed of other sounds", and the same goes for the verb.[9] "Diction" is one of the necessary six "parts" that constitute the peculiar character or quality of a tragedy. "The excellence of diction consists in being perspicuous without being mean."[10] The art of being "perspicuous", i.e. capable of expressing things clearly, is central to Eliot's conception of the objective correlative.

The poet can work with words: the language of tragedy should be "embellished and rendered pleasurable",[11] and "the greatest (sc. excellence) of all is to be happy in the use of metaphor; for it is this alone that cannot be acquired, and which, consisting in a quiet discernment of resemblances, is a certain mark of genius".[12]

The receiver makes a rare appearance in *Poetics*, and the work does not seem to cater for a specific group of recipients. However, the existence of a target group is obviously presupposed. "We" like successful imitations, it says on one of the first pages, and what would be the purpose of "embellishing" the presentation if it were not for the benefit of a recipient?

Poetics is a study of the creation of some literary genres, and it is an attempt to devise a system for 'poetry' as Aristotle knew it. In some respects, the treatise is also a list of prescriptions to a budding poet, and the large number of quotations of outstanding poets' achievements may serve as a guide to anyone who would like to try his hand at literary pursuits.

Discreet advice to the poet is scattered throughout the work: he must be a master of formulation so as to be able to render the presentation elegant, he must find words that are appropriate to the heroic deeds he depicts, he must never lose sight of the imitation aspect, and it is desirable that he should show some competence, if not "genius", in the handling of metaphor. Aristotle sees no rigid dividing line between epic poetry and tragedy in terms of content and form: they are both written in verse, and Aristotle is obviously attracted to metre, which is "plainly a species of rhythm".[13]

It is interesting, not least for the subject of this book, that this very early example of literary criticism should devote so much space to the language issue, more particularly to the use of words. The reason why they fascinate Aristotle is that words, according to him, have the capacity to imitate, and the purpose of epic poetry and tragedy is imitation. His copious exemplification shows that what he has in mind is not onomatopoeia, but metaphoric application of the everyday vocabulary. The aim for the 'maker' — the etymological meaning of 'poet' — should be to obtain precision and elegance.

Imitation, as Aristotle sees it, 'points outwards' — the phenomenon particularly worthy of imitation is heroic action, just as Eliot found that 'a scene' might be an appropriate objective correlative for a poet's reaction. Aristotle does not talk about an inward-looking reproduction of the workings of the poet's mind. Nor does Eliot.

Demetrius of Phalerum (c. 350–263 BC)

Demetrius was both a statesman and a philosopher, an enlightened governor of Athens, an an outstanding orator, and the author of many scholarly works, among them a treatise *On Style*, which is a mixture of stock-taking and advice to prospective poets and dramatists, i.e. in many respects similar to Aristotle's *Poetics*. Demetrius undertakes a detailed categorization of styles: the plain style, the polished style, the dignified style, etc. He dwells on sentences, especially with reference to their length, and on the choice of words suitable to each style. The treatise is the fruit of his own extensive reading, and the aim is to show how a listener or spectator — or perhaps a reader — (none of whom are ever referred to explicitly) can be influenced, impressed, or disgusted. For the benefit of the recipient, it is important that the diction be suited to the style, and Demetrius' work lives up to its title: it is a collection of stylistic figures and their effects. Metaphors and different metres are described at great length in terms of their contributions to the creation of a total effect. But also words are given a considerable amount of attention: the arrangement of words, the coining of new words, and the role of the individual word in the context are commented on. "A rough word produces a rough effect", says Demetrius.[14]

Horace

Horace's *Epistle to the Pisos*, better known as *Ars poetica*, was probably written around 19 BC. Addressed to a father and two sons, the letter contains advice to an aspiring poet, its emphasis being on the content of especially tragedy and epic poetry. Horace, too, follows in Aristotle's footsteps.

The idea of appropriateness, or correlation, where content is concerned, appears at the very start: neither in a painting nor in a poem should a horse's neck be united to a human head.

The work is impressionistic and allusive, anything but systematic. In *Essay on Criticism* (ll. 653–54), Pope gives a succinct characterization:

Horace still charms with graceful negligence,
And without method talks us into sense.

References to the recommended treatment of words occur
sporadically and always in the form of *obiter dicta* that are not
further elaborated. But that Horace was aware of the part played
by words is evidenced by statements like the following:

> Let the author of the proposed poem show taste and care in linking
> up his words; let him embrace one word and reject another. Your
> diction will be excellent if a clever combination renders a familiar
> word original.[15]

It is possible to read an allusion to metaphoric use of language
into that statement. Also, Horace is aware that "words perish with
old age, and others, newly born, thrive and flourish like youths".[16]
That opinion is difficult to reconcile with Eliot's conception of the
stability of word meanings.

And what, in Horace's view, were poets going to write about?
"I would advise the well-instructed imitator to take his model
from life and customs, and from this derive language faithful to
life."[17] So Horace acknowledges the mimetic principle, and the
imitandum was the world outside the poet, not what was going on
in his own mind. That attitude would be heartily endorsed by
Eliot.

As to the process of verbalization, Horace echoes Cato the
Elder's first rule for orators: "rem tene, verba sequentur". Horace
repeats the advice, in a slightly different formulation, in the same
passage as the previous quotation: "Words will quickly follow
when the matter is ready".[18] That is as far as this eminent critic
from Antiquity goes in the handling of the thorny problem of
accounting for the leap from impression to formulation.

CHAPTER TWO

SPRAT, LOCKE, HARTMANN

Thomas Sprat

In his *History of the Royal Society* (1667), Thomas Sprat pointed to the significance of the word for the written records of scientists. He paid tribute to

> the primitive purity and shortness when men deliver'd so many things almost in an equal number of words . . . Things lie in great number before the mind, awaiting arrangement and selection. The mind, on the other hand, is wholly separate from them: things can be clearly and distinctly separated from our continuous experience of them . . . What I experience governs all thought.[1]

The statement is in accordance with the Cartesian dichotomy, and at the same time anticipates the theory of Locke. Also, it will be seen, it is a declaration of content for Positivist scientists' outlook on "reality"

John Locke

An Essay Concerning Human Understanding, published in 1690 after 30 years of epistemological speculation, refutes the theory of innate ideas, the "establish'd Opinion amongst some Men, That there are in the Understanding certain Innate Principles . . . which the Soul receives in its very first Being, and brings into the World with it". Locke's often quoted dictum "nihil in intellectu quod non prius ín sensu" posits the existence of a something outside the sentient ego which is a determining factor for the operations of the human mind.

The content of our minds stems from sensory experience. Far from discussing the nature of 'reality', Locke points to the indispensability of our surroundings: without input from the outside world, man's mind would be a blank, a *tabula rasa* — apart from some instruments suitable for the reception and processing of sensory data, we must presume. Locke talks about mankind in general so the inference is that a poet, too, is dependent on 'the other' for his material.

The relevance of Locke's assumption for Eliot's theory of the objective correlative is obvious: sense data impact on the observant poet, whose special talent enables him to find 'le mot juste' to describe, characterize, or assess his sensory experience. Like Locke, Eliot not only presupposes the existence of 'reality', he also sees it as the poet's obligation to 'take it as it is' and not to 'improve' it or moralize on it, as for example the Neo-Classicists did.

Also, Locke's speculations on the 'nominal essence' of objects have some bearing on the subject dealt with in this book. According to Locke, the name we give an object represents our idea of that object. How such names come into existence remains obscure. However, some similarity can be detected with what lies at the root of Eliot's postulate about the objective correlative: by calling his reaction a name, the poet conjures up in the receiver's mind an image or an analogue of that reaction.

Hartmann

The conditions for giving verbal expression to feelings were
discussed by the German philosopher Edouard von Hartmann,
who, in his book *Philosophy of the Unconscious* (1869) takes the
Lockean position one step further: "only in so far as thoughts can
be already translated into words, only so far are they *communica-
ble*" (his italics).[2]

CHAPTER THREE

GAUTIER, BAUDELAIRE, GOURMONT

Gautier

It is a well-known fact that English art criticism towards the end of the 19ᵗʰ century and in the first two decades of the 20ᵗʰ century was heavily indebted to contemporary French theorists. One French critic who served as a source of inspiration to Eliot was Théophile Gautier (1811–72), whose reflections on language in general and 'le mot juste' in particular were of crucial significance to Eliot's supposition about the objective correlative.

Gautier began as art critic in 1832 with only minimal knowledge about pictorial principles. His critical oeuvre, covering a multitude of aspects of painting, sculpture, architecture, drama, and music, spans some forty years.[1] Economic necessity seems to have been the root cause of his prodigious output. He produced regular *Salon* articles, collected in three books from 1847, 1855, and 1861 respectively.

"One should not neglect the craft that is an essential part of every art form," he said in 1836.[2] The formal aspect of art was what fascinated him; the sculpture and architecture of Antiquity — categories of art where form is visible and palpable — delighted him,[3] and his manifest interest in painting largely concentrated on form. The title of his collection of poetry from 1852, *Emaux et Camées*, is meant to express, in his own words,

the plan of treating small subjects in a restricted form . . . Each
piece should be a locket . . . The author only used the eight-foot
verse, which he remelted, burnished and chased with all the care
of which he is capable.[4]

One of Gautier's axioms was that there is no idea which cannot
be expressed.[5] And in a conversation with Emile Bergerat he said:

the person who is surprised by a thought, be it ever so complex,
or by a vision, be it ever so apocalyptic, without having words to
express it, is not a writer.[6]

To Gautier, poetry is primarily a linguistic art form. Its object
was neither didactic nor mimetic, but to give a representation of
the ideal beauty that all artists contain within them. The indi-
vidual artist contemplates that ideal beauty through "the eyes of
the soul" in such a way that all that they see is subordinated to that
august concept.[7] By writing what occurs to him (ce qui lui vient à
la tête), the poet manages to create something that is better than
if he had slavishly copied the world around him. "When Mr.
Delacroix creates a picture, he looks into himself instead of placing
his nose at the window."[8]

In Gautier's perception, every poet should carry within him a
'microcosm', i.e. a diminutive perfect world from which he extracts
the thought and form of his work. So, unlike the Neo-Classicists,
to whom the ideal was outside the artist, to Gautier mimesis meant
a processed introspection. The stimulus came from outside, but it
was the poet's reservoir that enabled him to lick it into shape. To
Gautier, a suitable poetic subject was not a ransacking of the poet's
own mind.

In a review article from 1847 — the book being reviewed is
Rudolph Töpffer's *Réflexions et menus Propos d'un peintre genevois* —
Gautier elaborates on his theory:

A man who has not his inner world to translate is not an artist.

Imitation is the means and not the end. . . . However, it should not be concluded that the artist is purely subjective; he is also objective; he gives and he receives. He takes from nature the signs he needs in order to express it. Those signs he transforms: he adds or removes according to the type of his thinking . . . The painter carries his picture inside him, and the canvas serves as an intermediary between nature and himself.[9]

The Lockean echo is unmistakable: everything begins with sense impressions. However, Gautier proceeds beyond this initial stage. Once the signal has been received, the poet's imagination starts its operations: it 'translates' the input, gently bringing it into accordance with the components of the microcosm in the poet's mind. Admittedly, the ontological status of the microcosm and its ingredients, and how it all came into existence, remains unexplained. But Gautier is one of the few literary theorists who have acknowledged the verbalization problem, and who has dug one spit deeper in an attempt to explain the workings of the creative imagination.

The imagination is postulated to play a passive as well as an active role: a subject/object relationship is held to obtain between the outside world and the poet's mind. Before he delivers the result to his recipients, the poet has put his individual stamp on the original sense impression.

The conclusion drawn by Gautier is that the imagination is, at the same time, creator and judge. Thus poetry and criticism become complementary activities. Poetic creation is more than just a whisper from the Muse: it is the result of a conscious process, and it requires constant contributions from the poet's awareness and verbal competence.

Since he is a directly responsible participant in the process, it is incumbent on the poet not to be carried away by his passions. On the contrary, he should endeavour to control them. By the same token, the poet should practise incessant theoretical and methodological criticism of what he has created. Thus he will be able to achieve what is to Gautier the ultimate purpose of poetry, viz. the cultivation and encouragement of beauty.[10]

Baudelaire

Charles Baudelaire (1821–67) started his career at a time when Gautier was held in high esteem as a journalist and a man of letters. The two men met in 1845, and by 1851 they were on 'cher ami' and first-name terms. Baudelaire considered Gautier his mentor and dedicated his epoch-making poem *Fleurs du Mal* (1857) to Gautier. Baudelaire wrote two 'studies' (*Etudes*), i.e. long essays, about Gautier. The first came out in 1859, in the periodical *L'Artiste*, the second in 1861, in *Les Poètes français*.[11] In those two studies, Baudelaire in his tribute to Gautier indirectly gives expression to some elements of his own poetic credo.

It is evident that the formal aspect of poetry is Baudelaire's primary concern in the *Etudes*: he extols the balance and precision, the rigour bordering on mathematical exactitude, that he finds in Gautier's poems. Gautier always finds the right word, 'le mot juste', and the adequate image.

Baudelaire is impressed by Gautier's "constante recherche verbale" and his technical virtuosity as versifier: Gautier was always at pains to enrich the language, to extend its limits, so as to make it 'say more'.[12] Gautier's choice of words refers to all aspects of human activity and civilization. He includes terms from technology, science, and the arts; he coins neologisms and does not shrink from using archaisms and foreign words.

Baudelaire pays tribute to the originality of Gautier's vocabulary. Words are chosen for their suggestiveness and the inherent beauty of their sounds. Gautier's use of metaphors, unexpected associations and bold *rapprochements* contribute to creating a harmonious and rhythmical effect. In a reference to Greek statues, for example, Gautier talks about "la musique des formes humaines", and about Alboni, a celebrated singer, about whom he says, "mellifluousness bursts forth from his lips like vapour with a sound attached to it".[13]

Baudelaire is respectful towards Gautier's painstaking and meticulous labour with language: the poet, in filtering the language, cleans it. Thanks to his astounding linguistic command, Gautier was able to put even the most diminutive observation in its natural place without omitting any detail. All the time, Gautier's supreme mastery of language prompts "le mot propre, le mot unique" to spring forth, and the total effect is one of immaculate order.[14]

The encomia printed above should not be taken to mean that Baudelaire was unequivocally enthusiastic about Gautier's theories of art. Thus he was sceptical with regard to the latter's vagueness about 'ideal beauty', and he decidedly distanced himself from Gautier's strong attachment to religion. It is uncertain whether the two men met after 1859.

In his early career, Baudelaire was, by most critics, considered inferior to Gautier both as poet and as critic. However, later in the 19th century Baudelaire was rehabilitated by influential poets such as Verlaine, Rimbaud, Laforgue and the Symbolists.[15] By the early 20th century, Gautier's stature as an all-round critic was on the wane, but his linguistic theories and his poetical achievements helped to shape the manifestos, and determine the poetical output, of several schools of poets in the first two decades of the 20th century, e.g. the Imagists.

Gourmont

In the Preface to the 1928 edition of *The Sacred Wood*, Eliot acknowledges his debt to Remy de Gourmont (1858–1915) and expresses his gratitude for the inspiration he has received from the Frenchman's critical writings. Eliot calls Gourmont "the critical conscience of his generation".

Gourmont was one of the most brilliant and erudite minds of the period from 1885 to 1915.[16] Essentially an essayist and a critic, he took up the cudgels for the Symbolist movement, and for many years he was editor of the influential periodical *Mercure de France*. He was one of the leading figures in contemporary social, political, and literary debates. He held very pronounced views on democracy, capitalism, communism, socialism and Cabinet responsibility — he detested them all. When he died, Ezra Pound said, "Gourmont is dead, and the world's light is darkened".[17]

Gourmont's collected works amount to more than four volumes within the genres of science, linguistics, philosophy, and art criticism. His best works of literary criticism date from the years 1900 to 1915, the year of his death: *La Culture des Idées* (1900), *Le Problème du Style* (1902), and his collection of essays, *Promenades littéraires* and *Promenades philosophiques*, which appeared periodically from 1904 until after his death.

Gourmont was something of a polymath — artist, critic, philosopher and scientist, and his reflections on 'the great schism' caused by the Cartesian dichotomy in the early 17th century probably inspired Eliot's theory about the dissociation of sensibility. After Descartes, man had become divided against himself, and some contemporary poets (e.g. the Symbolists) attempted to make him whole again. That is what made Eliot embrace Symbolism, for the Symbolists refused to accept what they saw as Descartes' separation of Reason and Feeling. Gourmont, too, was sceptical towards the capability of reason to give a generally truthful representation of reality. If thought is, in actual fact, a physiological product that differs in quality and mode of operation from one individual to another, the world can be considered unknowable since each person will draw an individual image of what he or she sees.[18]

That postulate not only delivers a powerful blow to Positivist determinism. It also gives a free rein to an artist's originality.[19] Not surprisingly, Gourmont considers the complexity and obscurity of Symbolist art an asset. Gourmont is relevant in the context of the analysis performed in this book because he looked at style from a psychological as well as a verbal point of view. Nineteenth-century French philosophers and men of letters were pre-Freudians in that they were interested in psychology and psychiatry, thus Ribot's *Imagination créatrice* (1900) devotes many pages to a study of the unconscious.

Gourmont said,

> Who says style says visual memory and metaphoric power, combined in variable proportions with the emotional memory and all the obscure contributions of the other senses.[20]

His *Problème du Style* was written as a refutation of the theories of a certain M. Albalat, who had maintained that a budding writer could learn the profession by imitating famous authors' way of writing. After all, "les beautés littéraires sont fixes".[21] Gourmont thought that Albalat was barking up the wrong tree. His theories smacked of Neo-Classical imitation of authors from Antiquity, but Gourmont saw imitation as determined by the phenomenal world:

> All imaginative literature is based on reality. Science, too takes reality as the launching pad. The difference between the two is that literature is aware that it recasts when imitating.[22]

Gourmont agrees with the Lockean maxim "nihil in intellectu quod non prius in sensu":

> The senses are the only gateway through which everything that lives in the spirit has entered . . . an idea is nothing but a sensory experience stripped of its freshness.[23]

Like Gautier, Gourmont was fascinated by the mysterious process that transformed the initial sensation. Here he invoked the assistance of psychology and pointed to the part played by the subconscious; but he does not go into any great detail.[24]

However, he also saw a close connection between sensibility and intelligence, which meant that writing is to some extent governed by reason.

Gourmont repeatedly underlines the significance of what he calls the visual memory,

> this reservoir of images from which imagination draws its nourishment for the establishment of ever new and endless combinations.[25]

The poet is a privileged person who is endowed with a particular talent:

> It is an indisputable fact that there are men in whom every word conjures up a vision, and who have never adjusted the most imaginary description without having the exact model of it before his inner eye.[26]

We may here recall what Eliot said in *The Sacred Wood*: the poet's task is not to find new feelings, but to use the ordinary ones, and, in working them up into poetry, to express an emotion which is not in the actual feelings at all. And feelings which he has never experienced before will serve his turn as well as those familiar to him.

Gourmont was confident that the senses develop thanks to what he calls "life's natural education". So it is 'life', the storehouse which is the product of regularly occurring sensory input, which will create the image.[27] The similarity with Gautier's 'microcosm' is unmistakable, and Eliot's concept of tradition is not far away either, for the person who is able to verbalize an aesthetic emotion is determined by his heredity and education and thus becomes a 'maker' and, at the same time, the guardian of a tradition.

Pure poetry has nothing to do with the feelings, said Gourmont, and that postulate is heartily endorsed by Eliot:

The end of enjoyment of poetry is pure contemplation from which all accidents of personal emotion are removed.[28]

Burne puts it this way:

The intensity of the poetry is another thing again than the intensity of the experience which one attributes to the poet. Art requires *sang-froid*, which it is the nature of the emotions to make one lose.[29]

Like Gourmont, Eliot sees a radical difference between the man who suffers and the mind which creates. In *The Sacred Wood* he states that the more the two are separate,

the more perfectly will the mind digest and transmute the passions which are its material.[30]

The assumption is complementary to the concept of the objective correlative: the poet must, unsentimentally, specify his reaction in terms of 'the right word', and, analogously, the finished product, the work, must limit and circumscribe its own emotional potential. A "visual memory" combined with an "emotional memory" are, in Gourmont's opinion, two indispensable prerequisites for mastering the art of writing. However, more is needed: a competent poet must have the ability, when facing an object in the outside world, to "move back" to the emotional state that he sight originally aroused in him.[31]

To Gourmont, the content of literature is important, but content should always be adapted to, and subservient to, style. And thinking activity is a fundamental ingredient of style; without that basis, style is in a bad way.[32] Gourmont's formulation makes it clear that he did not take mimesis in the sense of slavish copying. "The logic of the eye and the logic of each of the other senses are sufficient".[33] So, the senses have a logic of their own, but their perceptions have to be approved and adjusted by the poet's visual and emotive memory. The inference is that mere copying would be impossible, for the need for scientific exactitude risked corrupting the evidence of the senses. That, by the way, was the reason why Gourmont found the discoveries of science dubious and problematic because they were hypothetical.

To Gourmont, words are "vitalized" by the feelings they evoke:

> Words only have meaning by the force of the feeling they involve and the representation of feeling conferred on them . . . Even the most sluggish words can be vitalized by the sensibility, they can become feelings . . . Every word, every turn of phrase, even proverbs and clichés, may for the emotive writer become nuclei of emotional crystallization.[34]

It is the interdependence of word and feeling that Gourmont finds intriguing. On the one hand, he maintains that the word should correspond exactly to the thought being expressed, but on the other he had to confess (e.g. in *La Rhétorique*) that

> words and sensations are in harmony only very rarely and very poorly.[35]

An individual way of seeing and feeling inevitably leads to an individual way of using language. Gourmont was aware that the meaning of words may vary from one man to another and from one moment to another with the same person. Therefore it may be difficult to get at an exact understanding of much writing.[36] His dilemma was that, on the other hand, he had no doubt that truth depended on words, and accordingly he studied the development and evolution of meaning indefatigably. He hoped that this approach would take him closer to the crystallizations of associations which words have acquired through the centuries; what he was aiming at was a kind of dictionary of associations.

In *The Perfect Critic*, Eliot complains of the instability and incredible vagueness of words. They are losing their concreteness because we tend to substitute emotion for thought. Gourmont exerted a huge influence on Eliot. The structure, sometimes the very formulation, of much of Eliot's literary criticism is heavily indebted to the Frenchman. Eliot used quotations from Gourmont as epigraphs for section headings in *The Sacred Wood*. He agreed with Gourmont that sensuous impressions are the basis of literary activity and that the input, after being recast in the poet's crucible, should be given a formulation that would satisfy the criterion of literary beauty. The theory of the dissociation of sensibility is borrowed from Gourmont, who talked about "dissociation of ideas", and who wanted to take ideas back to their origin in sensory experience.

Eliot actually echoes Gourmont when, in the essay on Chapman,[37] he talks about "a direct sensuous apprehension of thought". The fact the Eliot became interested in the poet Laforgue's poems and refers to him respectfully in central passages of his criticism, is largely due to Gourmont, who admired Laforgue because, in the latter's poetry intelligence was closely connected with sensibility.

Eliot pays tribute to Laforgue for the same reason as Gourmont: he was possessed of an astounding linguistic inventiveness, and in his poetry as well as in Baudelaire's and Corbière's poems he finds the same

essential quality of transmuting ideas to sensation, of transforming an observation into a state of mind.[38]

And the reason why the Elizabethan dramatists captivated him was that, in their work, "sensation becomes word".[39]

Ultimately, the postulate about the dissociation of sensibility derives from the philosopher F.H. Bradley, about whom Eliot had written an unpublished doctoral dissertation.[40] Eliot found Bradley's argumentation and reasoning a useful criterion for evaluating the achievements of not only 17th century dramatists, but also the works of some of his own contemporaries.

Like Gourmont, although to a lesser degree, Eliot was concerned with the role of the unconscious in the creative process. Gourmont, however, cast his net wider than Eliot: to all intents and purposes, our moral and aesthetic judgements are nothing but unconscious generalizations of sensations, and potentially valueless without the correcting and sobering influence of intelligence. But Eliot agreed wholeheartedly with Gourmont in the latter's banning of 'personality' as a determining factor in the process of creation. And the critic was told to beware: only such emotions as are immediately provoked by the work under consideration should be granted access to the critic's assessment.[41]

However, there were several points where Eliot gradually came to oppose Gourmont's radical stance. For one thing, Gourmont was avowedly hostile to religion and religion-based morality, about which Eliot was certainly not. Consequently, in matters of sin and justice the two men were separated by an abyss.[42] Nor did Eliot share Gourmont's black pessimism on the subject of society and politics.

CHAPTER FOUR

POSITIVISM AND SOME REACTIONS AGAINST IT

Positivism is defined by OED as follows:

> A system of philosophy elaborated by Auguste Comte, which
> recognizes only positive facts and observable phenomena, with
> the objective relations of these and the laws which determine
> them, abandoning all inquiry into causes or ultimate origins;
> also, a religious system founded upon this philosophy, in which
> the object of worship is Humanity considered as a single corpo-
> rate being.

Since Watt patented his invention of the steam engine in 1769,
technological inventions had, as the 19th century progressed, trans-
formed not only most people's world view, but also their everyday
lives. Especially in the latter half of the century, the working
methods of science and the results yielded by the way they formu-
lated their questions acquired enormous prestige.

The determining factor of the Positivist paradigm was quan-
tification: counting, weighing, and measuring were felt to be able
to give answers that were immediately graspable by common
sense, and the validity of the "natural laws" that were deduced was
confirmed by their seeming incontestability. The consequence was
that the results obtained by science obtained truth value: truth

came to mean accordance with "what you could lay your hands on". What had to do with objects became of central relevance to the Positivists. Objectivity became a key concept to them. It was not only a working method, it was also an attitude to what was outside the observer, and it was a guarantor of truth.

The ultimate aim of the Positivists was to give a reliable and incontrovertible description of reality, and science seemed to have the tools to provide it. Even if the data were collected by human beings and processed by human minds, subjectivity became a derogatory term, relegated to the level of sheer whimsicality.

The word Positivism was coined in the late 18th century by the Frenchman Saint-Simon (1760–1825). His pupil Auguste Comte (1798–1857) used the designation about the way of thinking he would like to introduce into philosophy. Comte was confident that "the march of civilization" is subject to an unchangeable law based on "the way things are".[1] And he underlined that the Positivist spirit endeavours to determine the how, not the why.[2] He based his philosophical thinking on a belief in progress: history moves through a series of phases, from a lower to the highest level, which is the Positivist approach.

Leaning on Newtonian physics, prominent scientists like Lord Kelvin (1824–1907) claimed that the "natural laws" that they had discovered gave an adequate and irrefutable image of reality. Their claim was supported by the large number of technological inventions that made everyday life easier for the common man.

Positivists were satisfied that there is such a thing as universal truth. Truth is one, they said, and our picture of it has general validity, witness the reliability of the natural laws we have discovered. These laws simply demonstrate and reflect the order of the universe.

However, the question of "why" could not so easily be brushed aside. In *First Principles* (1862–93), Herbert Spencer admitted that many of the abstract and technical terms used by scientists, e.g. motion, were actually nothing but convenient labels.[3] The point implicitly made by Spencer is that science has to resort to metaphorical language to account for its theories, which makes their ontological status dubious.

The insufficiency of the Positivist paradigm was becoming increasingly obvious, not least where areas outside natural science were concerned. The art historian and literary critic Hippolyte Taine had to resort to a metaphysical concept, viz. "la faculté maîtresse", to give an exhaustive explanation of the creation of a successful work of literature. Measurable phenomena like "la race, le milieu et le moment" obviously did not suffice. The Neo-Classicists had found themselves in the same quandary, so they hid behind the "je ne sais quoi".

Herbert Spencer blamed contemporary science for falling short on crucial issues like the nature of the First Cause, and Positivist philosophers, moralists, theologians and what we would today call sociologists, had a feeling that there must be "something" above or behind what observation and the consequent establishment of smooth-fitting laws could teach us.[4]

Eliot's teacher at Harvard, the philosopher Francis Herbert Bradley (1846–1924), was what could be called with an oxymoron a systematic metaphysician. He saw it as the goal of philosophy to create a rational system of first principles. He acknowledges the existence of "our real world", which, he held, is not a figment of somebody's imagination or merely a fictional concept. He proved the actual existence of "our real world" by stating that

> either in endeavour to deny it, or even in attempting to doubt it, we tacitly assume its validity.[5]

In Bradley's idiolect, "our real world" is something different from "reality", which is an abstract term, viz. the ultimate logical subject of all acts of judgement.[6] As will be seen, that is a view poles apart form that of the Positivists.

In *Appearance and Reality* (1893), Bradley's thesis is that "our real world" is not susceptible of description in terms of time, space, causation or movement — another serious blow to the Positivist conception. Bradley's generally sceptic theory has metaphysical overtones, and he was led to the conclusion that ultimate truth is unobtainable, for we humans are not provided with the necessary tools to understand "the nature of things". The best we can hope for is a small number of unconditional truths about the most general features of "our real world".

Bradley considered the relation between thought and "our real world" a major philosophical problem. Language was not his prime concern, but in his usage, 'thought' was virtually inseparable from 'language'. The idea echoes Hegel's proposition that

> the forms of thought are, in the first instance, displayed and stored in human *language*. (his italics)[7]

In his explanation of the activities of the unconscious, Bradley divides the mind into levels. The first and uppermost level is what he calls "immediate experience", by which he understands visual stimulus, or a feeling. "Immediate experience", accompanied by pleasure or pain, is an undeniable feature of human and animal life, for which reason Bradley ascribes truth value to it. The problem for Bradley was to find out how thought and language respectively were capable of dealing with such a phenomenon as immediate experience.[8] He had no doubt that reason has a fundamental part to play in the processing of "immediate experiences", and it will be seen that Eliot followed in his teacher's footsteps.

Positivism was becoming gradually more vulnerable because its paradigm failed to bridge the gap between nature and spirit; slowly its adversaries acquired a greater degree of self-assurance and cogency. And very soon after the turn of the century they got a helping hand from an unexpected corner: Einstein's theories, propounded in 1905 and later, eventually shattered the Positivist conception of reality.

During the first two decades of the 20th century, we witness, on the part of poets, philosophers and critics, increasing efforts to challenge the monopoly of the Positivist world picture. Surely, reality, and, more generally, life, could not be described exclusively in terms of weighing, counting, and measuring? The opposition originated in France, where it became particularly vocal. Critics such as Ribot, Gautier and Gourmont advocated for a breakaway from the prevalent straitjacket, and poets like Baudelaire, Laforgue and Mallarmé experimented with hitherto untried poetical forms. Since they wanted to illuminate rather than to describe or to narrate, the emphasis came to be on formal aspects, more specifically the use and function of the individual word and the effects of rhythm.

> Poets in 1910 inherited a world made out of words . . . coherence was obtained by exploiting the sounds of the words and the implications concealed in their sounds,

says Hugh Kenner.[9]

The reason why those reformist tendencies caught on in England is twofold: English poetry from the two decades straddling the year 1900, as represented by for example Alfred Noyes and Henry Newbolt, was decidedly lightweight and flabby with outworn subjects, where sentiment often degenerated into sentimentality, characterized by humdrum rhythms, straitjacket-like metres, and a dull and watered down poetic diction. And literary criticism from the same period had virtually nothing to offer in the way of theoretical discussion.

A group of devoted young poets, who in most cases were also critics (Aldington, Eliot, Fletcher, Flint, Ford, H.D., Hulme, Lewis and Pound) made their voices heard in an undergrowth of manifestos and periodicals, notably *The Egoist*. For some years after 1917, Eliot was editor of that periodical.

This group devoted a considerable amount of energy to discussions of formal criteria. The role of the individual word in the formation of the successful image was naturally prioritized. In their poems, the group members broke new ground: their poems were non-stanzaic, unrhymed, and characterized by sharpness of observation in the use of images. Their poems are neither narrative nor didactic; they are momentary snapshots of everyday scenes frozen in one or two images. The task the poets set themselves was not to write a traditionally 'beautiful' poem, but rather to create what they called a 'successful' one.

CHAPTER FIVE

THE OBJECTIVE
CORRELATIVE

The Theory

The only way of expressing emotion in the form of art is by finding an "objective correlative": in other words, a set of objects, a situation, a chain of events which shall be the formula of that *particular* emotion such that when the external facts, which must terminate in sensory experience, are given, the emotion is immediately evoked. If you examine any of Shakespeare's more successful tragedies, you will find this exact equivalence; you will find that the state of Lady Macbeth walking in her sleep has been communicated to you by a skilful accumulation of imagined sensory impressions . . . .The artistic "inevitability" lies in this complete adequacy of the external to emotion, and this is precisely what is deficient in *Hamlet*. Hamlet (the man) is dominated by an emotion which is inexpressible because it is in excess of the facts as they appear.[1]

This frequently quoted but rarely analysed passage occurs in the essay *Hamlet* written in 1919. It was printed in the collection *The Sacred Wood*, the first edition of which came out in 1920. In the revised edition from 1969, the title of the re-edited essay is *Hamlet and his Problems*, but this central passage has not been changed.

Eliot said himself that it is important to put a date on his critical statements since he was liable to modify or transform his opinions from time to time. Therefore, it is relevant to point out that the formulation is admitted unchanged and without any further elaboration in the later editions of the essay. Add to this, the late twenties are a crucial period in Eliot's intellectual development; those are the years when he made his attitude to central issues clear: a classicist in literature, a royalist in politics, and an Anglo-Catholic in religion, Actually, 1928 is the year of his religious conversion.

In the essay, Eliot calls *Hamlet* an artistic failure because the protagonist's reaction is disproportionate to the situation in which he finds himself:

> Hamlet is up against the difficulty that his disgust is occasioned by his mother, but that his mother is not an adequate equivalent for it, his disgust envelops and exceeds her.[3]

Eliot's treatment of Shakespeare's play may seem idiosyncratic, but the statement just quoted is a natural preparation for the more general point he is making in the essay: Gertrude's behaviour is not an appropriate objective correlative for Hamlet's emotions.

Language

Eliot never tires of stressing the importance for a poet to study and learn to master language:

> A ceaseless care, a passionate and untiring devotion to language, is the first conscious concern of the poet.[4]

In *The Use of Poetry and the Use of Criticism* he calls for "correctness of expression" in contemporary poetry,[5] and he had full confidence in the capacity of language to present the object, to be so close to the object that the two are identified.[6]

The poet has a responsibility towards his language in terms of preservation, improvement, and extension.[7] Characteristically, in his essays dealing with renowned persons past and present, Eliot devotes at least as much space to their mastery of language as to the qualities for which they are traditionally famous. In *For Lancelot Andrewes* (1927), Eliot pays tribute to Niccolo Machiavelli because

> first of all he was concerned with truth, not with persuasion, which is one reason why his prose is great prose, not only of Italian, but a model of style for any language.[8]

In the same collection of essays, Francis Bradley, Eliot's respected and beloved philosophy mentor, is complimented for his style, which is "perfectly welded with the matter": the objective correlative, as exemplified by Bradley, we must understand, makes for a felicitous coalescence of word and object.[9] Bradley's care for words is repeatedly referred to in the essay:

> Bradley, like Aristotle, is distinguished for his scrupulous respect for words, that their meaning should be neither vague nor exaggerated.[10]

The Poet's Role

Eliot chooses an impersonal formulation for his thesis. He does not say, "A poet's only way . . ." because, to him, the poet's personality is of minor importance. In *Tradition and the Individual Talent* he says that "the progress of an artist is a . . . continual extinction of personality".[11] And later in the same essay we read that

> my meaning is, that the poet has, not a 'personality' to express.

but a particular medium, which is only a medium and not a personality, in which impressions and experiences combine in peculiar and unexpected ways.[12]

The reason why Eliot rejected realist drama was that it relies so heavily on the personality of the actor.[13] The sense impressions that the poet receives have truth value, and the poet is a transforming catalyst rather than a spontaneous creator. The poet's I and his emotions prompted by the phenomenal world are connected to that world with a strong bond. Accordingly, it is beside the point for the poet to "feel greatly" in preparation for composing a "great" poem.[14] One of Eliot's grievances against Matthew Arnold was that the latter put the emphasis in the wrong place, viz. on the poet's feelings.

In a discussion of Milton's *Lycidas*, Eliot says:

The more perfect the artist, the more completely separate in him will be the man who suffers and the mind which creates; the more perfectly will the mind digest and transmute the passions which are its material.[15]

In the essay *Four Elizabethan Dramatists* from 1924, Eliot states that "no artist produces great art by a deliberate attempt to express his personality",[16] and the gist of his dissatisfaction with *Hamlet* is that the protagonist is dominated by an emotion "which is in excess of the facts as they appear".[17]

It is worthy of notice that Eliot does not talk about an 'adequate' or an 'original' correlative. By using the term 'objective' he exploited the respectful connotations still surrounding science and its findings. Like many of his contemporary poets and critics, he aimed at obtaining parity of esteem between an objectified emotion and a scientific achievement. The resulting equivalent is held to have a status comparable to that of the objects that were science's field of study.

The Dissociation of Sensibility

In passages like those just quoted we find part of the explanation of Eliot's theory of the dissociation of sensibility. Kenner takes this use of the word 'sensibility' to be synonymous with the Bradleyan 'immediate experience', which precedes, underlies, and prompts any degree of analysis.

Eliot pays tribute to Chapman, who amalgamated learning and feeling in his dramas, and Ben Jonson as dramatist is rehabilitated by Eliot on that score.[18] Lancelot Andrewes, Bishop of Winchester, who died in 1526, seems to personify Eliot's ideal of poetic activity: in him, intellect and sensibility were in harmony:

> Andrewes's emotion is purely contemplative, it is not personal, it is wholly evoked by the object of contemplation, to which it is adequate; his emotion is wholly contained in and explained by its object.[19]

The thought and the terminology are clearly recognizable from Eliot's presentation of his objective correlative theory.

However, it is Eliot's contention that, after Ben Jonson, thought and feeling were separated, and thinking was no longer felt to be the province of poetry. In the centuries down to his own age Eliot sees increasing degeneration because poets' feelings and idiosyncrasies are given a free rein, thus excluding an essential element from poetry. Eliot talks repeatedly about "unity of sentiment", which he sees as a justification of the unity of action in a drama.

What Eliot attempted to do with his postulate of the objective correlative was to reinstate the intellectual aspect in its proper place. Thus, the objective correlative assertion becomes a natural corollary of his speculations about the dissociation of sensibility. The creation of poetry requires a fusion of feeling and intellect, and for that fusion to succeed, the poet's rational faculty, which Bradley calls "the principle of synthesis",[20] must play an active part. Bradley goes a step further in his long essay *The Presuppositions of Critical History*:

> Knowledge is the reception of outward impressions, and it is but natural that the copy should resemble and reproduce the original.[21]

Feeling and Emotion

In *Tradition and the Individual Talent*, Eliot establishes a distinction between feeling and emotion, feeling being sensations and impressions prompted by the immediate sensorial input. Emotion is a superordinate term, referring to the situation where intelligence has been brought to bear on feeling. It should be added, though, that the distinction is not consistently maintained by Eliot. For instance, he says in *The Sacred Wood* (1960, repr. 1969)[22] that poetry is not a *turning loose* of emotion, but a *turning away* from emotion. Here, emotion seems to be synonymous with feeling.

Be that as it may, in the objective correlative passage Eliot uses the term emotion with a specific sense: the context shows that the reference is to feeling with an intellectual component added. Feelings need to be clarified by the intellect, and the end-result of the successful blend of the two is emotion, a state of mind rather than an instance of, for example, anger or sadness. The poet's task, then, is to find an exact verbal equivalent for the emotion. and for that purpose it is incumbent on him

> not to find new emotion, but to use the ordinary ones, and, in making them up into poetry, to express feelings which are not in actual emotions at all.[23]

The formulation is not crystal clear; for example, the ontological status of 'intelligence' is obscure, and the distinction between feeling and emotion is not strictly maintained., but a description of the process may be formulated as follows:

The creative process begins in the personal experience: sense impressions, familiar ones as well as unfamiliar ones, we may take it, are registered, and thanks to the assistance and regulating influence of the intellect, the initial stimulus is filtered and stripped of its baser matter, which could be imagined to be part of the recipient's spontaneous reaction. The thinking activity is not that of the scientist or the logician. The point for the poet is to get "some order into his own instinctive reactions", as John Middleton Murry puts it. In that way the thought becomes "systematized emotion".[24]

Eliot admired Dante's *Divina Commedia* because he found it " the most *ordered* presentation of emotion that has ever been made"[25] (his italics). And in Bradley Eliot found support for the idea of the objectivity of thought: thought is objective

> not because its content excludes the self, but because it has to control tendencies which fall outside itself.[26]

Eliot had no doubt that the entire mental process was subject to control:

> That which suffers control is the entire psychical process . . . Sensations, emotions, fancies, volitions are suppressed or modified to suit the end, viz. to promote the development of the object.[27]

The fusion is worked into what Eliot calls an emotion, for which the poet rummages his mind, his visual memory and his verbal reservoir to find a suitable equivalent. Eliot views the process as a simple, almost mechanical operation, natural to the privileged person in whom the phenomenal world triggers a response, and who can draw on his reservoir — reminiscent of Gautier's *microcosme* — to furnish a truthful illustration of his reaction in the shape of "a set of objects, a situation, a chain of events".

The Implications

In order to get closer to an understanding of what Eliot was driving at, it is necessary to look into the implications of his categorical statement. The objective correlative is something from "our real world", i.e. outside the poet. Eliot took considerable interest in the unconscious, and he considered that introspection might in a few cases be a useful tool to try to account for some mental operations. Yet, even if he was not as suspicious of introspection as were the Positivists, he found that the results of introspection were not suitable for poetical treatment. So, the equivalence invoked, the basis of comparison, would be delivered by somebody or something else than the poet — even if it was he who pointed out the equivalence.

The correlative is not a word, or a synonym for an emotion. It is a context ("a set of objects . . . "). Eliot did not question Bradley's assumption that the immediate sense impressions had truth value; and Eliot extrapolated the truth value to hold for objective correlatives, too. The adjective 'objective' is a reminiscence of the thinking of the Positivists, to whom objectivity was synonymous with truth. The accordance revealed between the poet's emotion and the scene, etc., depicted, had truth value. It is not stipulated that that scene, etc., should have what is conventionally known as 'poetic' overtones.

The significant point is that, as Eliot sees it, truth can best be approached in a figurative way, through the use of one or more images. That is an echo of the Imagist conviction. They contested the Positivist pretention that truth was one, and that their working methods secured an unambiguous account of what the world was really like.

Eliot expressly distances himself from the Wordsworthian "emotion recollected in tranquillity":

For it is neither emotion, nor recollection, nor, without distortion of meaning, tranquillity.

Rather it is

> a concentration of a very great number of experiences . . . which
> does not happen consciously or of deliberation.[28]

To Locke, the mind was originally a *tabula rasa*, and Bradley
was almost just as categorical:

> In the beginning, there is nothing beyond what is presented, what
> is and is felt, or rather is felt simply. There is no memory or imag-
> ination or hope or fear or thought or will, and no perception of
> difference or likeness, no relations and no feelings, only feeling.[29]

Eliot does not conceal the fact that the composition of a poem
is, to a very great extent, a conscious undertaking, and the veracity
of the objective correlative becomes for the poet a tool to obtain
the "systematized order" that he desired. Emotion and intellect
undergo a kind of cross-fertilization: the sensory input influences
what is already 'there' in the poet's mind, but it is, in its turn, puri-
fied by the ingredients of the poet's mind.

It will be seen that the creative process implied in Eliot's postu-
late bears no little resemblance to what, according to Eliot,
happens when the emergence of a new poem sets its mark on the
existing tradition, which becomes modified, be it ever so slightly.

What lies behind Eliot's theory is his awareness of the fact that
most emotional reactions are notoriously insufficiently accounted
for by synonyms or dictionary definitions. The remedy he suggests
is for the poet to move into a different kind of presentation ("a situ-
ation") to give a satisfactory idea of the result of the fusion. The
outcome is the poet's victory over language, "compelling language
to conform to his mode of experience".[30] Thus it could be plausibly
argued — and the example is not Eliot's — that a person will get
a far more vivid picture of what jealousy 'is' by reading *Othello* than
by looking up the word in a dictionary of synonyms.

The Unconscious

Eliot refers to the quality and function of the unconscious on several occasions. The unconscious is the locus of impulses and feelings, but it also contains various ingredients of the conscious.[31] It is the mysterious starting-place of the creative process. Eliot talks about

> the dark embryo within him (sc. the poet) which gradually takes on the form and speech of the poem,[32]

and in *The Three Voices of Poetry* we read that a poem begins in

> an unknown dark psychic material — we might say the octopus or angel with which the poet struggles.[33]

Seen in that light, the objective correlative is what manages to bring the result of the 'dark' activities into light. However, Eliot never goes into detail with regard to the process of amalgamation that is postulated to take place between feeling and intellect.

Once more, Eliot got his inspiration from Bradley, who had proposed an analogous theory about the operations of the mind in his essay *The Presuppositions of Critical History* from 1887:

> But the mind is such a unity that it holds a contradiction in itself until the divided elements cohere, are solved and blended into another consciousness, a fresh system, a new world — new and which contains the old in a transformed shape . . . The mind is a principle of unity.[34]

The Example

Eliot's example of the objective correlative — and he gives only one — is taken from drama, viz. Lady Macbeth's state of mind in her sleepwalking scene. Perhaps Eliot chose to take his illustration from drama because the correlation will be more easily comprehensible to a reader or spectator on the basis of the actress's speeches and general pattern of behaviour.

However, the weakness of the postulate is that Eliot does not make it clear whether he refers to the poet's expressing himself precisely, or whether the point is the potential reader's reaction. Anyway, the question of the suitability of his example inevitably arises. At first sight, it may seem paradoxical that accuracy of formulation should be a virtue where emotions are concerned. But it is a natural corollary of the Positivist and Imagist craving for mathematical exactitude when a poet committed his reactions to a scene to paper. It is a well-known fact that the New Critics saw ambiguity or irony as the ultimate goal of a poetic presentation.

It is difficult to reconcile Eliot's italicized formulation, "that *particular* emotion" with the reactions that the Lady's behaviour will provoke in a spectator or a reader. What it does show is that there is not necessarily a one-to-one correspondence between stimulus and response. She is obviously thrown off her balance owing to the turn events have taken, but as to the *particular* emotion, various options seem to be open: the Aristotelian *katharsis*, i.e. mixture of pity ('What a deplorable state she finds herself in now') and fear ('The consequences turn out to be frightful when you push another person to commit a murder'). It could also be a feeling of just retribution ('She got what she deserved'), or even relief ('At last justice is done').

Eliot does not give any specimens of objective correlatives from poetry; on the whole, he refers only very sporadically to the theory in his critical oeuvre. But the theory, for all its ambiguity, is not without relevance: we might point to the famous description of his crossing of the Alps made by John Dennis (1657–1724): the emotion objectified is *the poet's* state of mind in the presence of the sublime, viz. fascination by the beauty, and horror at the forbidding enormity, of the scene. Another instance might be Wordsworth's poem *Lucy Gray* which prompts a feeling of

Aristotelian *katharsis in the recipient* — pity with the poor little girl, and fear at the cruelty of the fate that is liable to befall even completely innocent human begins. In neither case is it a *particular* emotion.

The innumerable examples in English literature of "Ode to . . . ", or "Ode on . . ." present the matter more succinctly seen from the poets' point of view: they have stated what emotion they want to focus on. Elegies strike a mood in their very titles.

Eliot asserts that his postulate is valid for all arts, which means that composers, sculptors, painters and choreographers use a non-verbal medium to project and objectify their emotions. Again, as in the case of literature, titles are helpful, but not unequivocal. Portraits may be intended to, and manage to, prompt mixed responses from beholders. What does Leonardo's *La Gioconda*'s smile suggest? Even compositions within the category of programme music are open to various interpretations: is Tschaikovsky's 1812 overture *only* a battle cry of triumph? And who will be prepared to give a final verdict on the mood of Mozart's symphonies?

Reality

Eliot's reflections in the crucial passage evidently hark back to Locke, but it is Locke with a grain of salt. Locke took the world outside man, *physis* in the Greek sense of the word, lock, stock, and barrel. It was *there* as an indisputable fact, and it sent signals for man to decipher. "Reality" is a precondition for the activities of the human mind. The impact of the facts of the outside world causes them to terminate in sensory experience, and to prompt a response on the part of a recipient.

To Eliot, the case is a little more problematic: he shares Locke's interest in, and respect for, "reality". Yet he does not commit himself to any definite standpoint with regard to man's position *vis-à vis* that entity:

The genesis of the common world can only be described by
admitted fictions . . . On the one hand, our experiences are similar
because they are of the same objects, and on the other hand the
objects are only 'intellectual constructions' out of various and
quite independent experiences. So, on the one hand my experience
is in principle public. My emotion may be better understood by
others than by myself; as my oculist knows my eyes. And on the
other hand everything, the whole world, is private to myself,

he wrote in a comment on Bradley's philosophy.[35]

The problem that Eliot brings up here but does not pursue is
this: what is the true character of the phenomenal world? How is
it to be understood? Is "reality" simply something that pre-exists
anything else, something on the status of which there is universal
agreement so that all people who watch it will get the same impres-
sion? Or is it an intellectual, man-made construction, a product of
man's reflections and his language? And what is the relationship
between man and the phenomenal world?

Disagreement on that essential issue has been a recurrent
phenomenon in the speculations and discussions of philosophers,
poets, moralists, scientists and religious people down through the
centuries.

In *Genesis* (II, 20) we read that

Adam gave names to all the cattle, to the fowl of the air, and to
every beast of the field,

i.e. reality was created by God, who made cosmos out of chaos. Man
was a later creation and was endowed with the privilege of putting
a name on the items which were already there. If "reality" is an
awe-inspiring edifice created by the Almighty it can *ipso facto*,
claim man's unquestioning veneration.

Kant dismisses the problem of "reality" in his *De mundi sensi-
bilis atque intelligibilis forma et principiis* from 1770. He establishes
time and space as *a priori* phenomena, 'Anschauungsformen',

which precede any kind of experience, and are not deduced from it. Reality must be considered as the 'something' which is the causal origin of a subject's sensations. Objects of experience conform to man's conceptions, for which reason it is impossible to say anything about an object 'before' or 'behind' experience since the idea of the object is created by a perceiving subject and thus governed by laws of concept formation. Accordingly, what we call "reality" has *a priori* existence, but Kant does not involve God in his reflections.

Eliot sits on the fence, but he agrees that in order to be able to communicate his impressions more precisely than one word can do, the poet has to invoke the assistance of an already existing 'something' outside him.

The tenor of the objective correlative passage in is perfect accordance with Imagist theorems, indeed they might be copied from one of the numerous manifestos that saw the light of day in the first decade of the 20th century. A poet like T.E. Hulme, for whom Eliot repeatedly expressed his admiration, demonstrated how observations of everyday life are capable of triggering a receptive poet's image-creating faculty without activating his emotional *engagement*. The poems of Hulme and the other Imagists are short, often a mere handful of lines, because their point is not to tell a story but rather to see and convey a scene '*à travers un tempérament*'. The poem *is* the image, and poetry is not a gushing forth of the poet's emotional qualms. Poets and critics looked upon poetry not in terms of applied ornament, but in terms of veracity, or 'successfulness' as they tended to call it. In their perception, veracity or truthfulness was obtained if and when their images reflected a valid identification with what they saw.[36]

Le mot juste

Gautier had pointed out that the criterion for the success of a formulation in, for example, a poem was that the author had managed to find 'the right word'. The teaching of F.H. Bradley at Harvard left its stamp not least on Eliot's attitude to words and language. Eliot came to see an intimate connection between the precise use of words in a philosophic or scientific analysis of the world and the precise treatment of words in a poem. A successful poetic description is a profitable and pleasurable contribution to a description of the world. And in *Knowledge and Experience in the Philosophy of F.H. Bradley*,[37] Eliot insists on the unity and conformity of feeling and objectivity.

Bradley had called Eliot's attention to the linguistic studies of thinkers like Russell, Whitehead, and Wittgenstein.[38] According to Russell, language is only used with precision when dealing with sensory experience. A logically perfect language must observe a one-to-one correspondence between each word and the thing or relationship it describes. Eliot was deeply impressed by Russell and Whitehead's *Principia mathematica* (1910–13), which he considered a greater contribution to linguistics than to mathematics. In *Tractatus* (1922) Wittgenstein said that the world is a totality of facts, and that each word unit must correspond to an object or an event in the world if the world is to have any meaning at all. Contemporary structuralism within linguistics was concerned with the relationship between language and object, as is seen in for example the works of the internationally famous Danish "grammatologist" Louis Hjelmslev. As he saw it, the relationship was one of pure logic, and ultimately it would be possible to calculate it by means of a system of equations (*Prolegomena to a Theory of Language*, 1961). Charles Peirce's philosophic realism implied that our thoughts about the world are not phenomena that are separated from or above the world, but derived from it: man's capacity to comprehend the mechanism of nature springs from his origin in that same nature. Man's mind is shaped under the influence of phenomena that are governed by mechanical laws. Consequently, some concepts that are imbedded in those laws are implanted in the mind, a fact that makes the laws easily comprehensible. Scientific theories express real knowledge of reality — that which Kant called *das Ding an sich* (*Reasoning and the Logic of Things*, 1992).

A different angle of approach to the significance of the word was taken by the orientalist Ernest Fenollosa (b. 1853), who was eulogized by Pound, but whose central work few contemporaries (or later theorists) seem to have actually read. Shortly before his premature death, in 1908, of a heart attack, he wrote a long seminal essay called *The Chinese Character as a Medium for Poetry*, in which he advised Anglo-Saxon poets to adopt the technique of the Chinese pictogram in their exploitation of metaphor.[39]

Thanks to what Middleton Murry calls his "personal idiosyncrasy of expression",[40] an Imagist poet — and Eliot was closely affiliated with several of the Imagists — becomes a 'maker', which is the etymological meaning of the word 'poet': the Greek verb *poiein* means 'make' or 'create'. Aristotelian mimesis was revitalized in the sense that the poet saw his task as being that of imitating. But the Imagists' imitation was a far cry from that of the Neo-Classicists: the latter strove to obtain the standards set by Homer and Horace, whereas Eliot and many of his contemporaries sought to grasp and communicate the essence of what met their eyes. A complete poem was a genuine and idiosyncratic rendering of 'the way things are'; the poet's concern was to show rather than to tell, not to win over the reader.

The Recipient

Towards the end of the theoretical part of the objective correlative passage, Eliot appears as the recipient of the poet's message. The latter does not play a prominent part in the context, but "the emotion immediately evoked" must refer to the response of the poet's opposite number, viz. the reader.

Eliot was satisfied that a relationship, common to all mankind, exists between a physical thing and a mental event. The mental events described by psychology are "probably not independent of the physical things to which they refer", as Shaff quotes him as saying.[41] Accordingly, he found it plausible that a reader's reaction will coincide with the intended aim of the author. In *The Use of Poetry and the Use of Criticism* he declares that the poetic experience presupposes the organization of various concrete experiences[42] (a favourite idea with Eliot), and he hoped that the reader would pass from selection and consequent discarding of what is useless to him, to an organization, perhaps a reorganization, of his mind. The exceptional reader will be able to compare and clarify, and in such cases enjoyment becomes appreciation. But what is supposed to give the reader that enjoyment is not necessarily the meaning of the text — actually some poets create intensity by ignoring meaning.[43]

In *Poetry and Drama* Eliot writes:

> If your poem is right to you, you can only hope the readers will eventually come to accept it . . . The approval of a few sympathetic and judicious critics is enough to begin with; and it is for future readers to meet the poet more than halfway.[44]

That rather intransigent take-it-or leave-it attitude is modified on the same page, for Eliot admits that a dramatist is forced to ensure understanding on the part of his audience. He saw it as "a function of art" (not *the* function) to force a structure on the disorderly chaos of reality.[45] When presented with that structure as reflected in a literary work, the reader may be inspired to play the poet's game, perhaps even move into areas where the poet cannot take him. But the responsibility rests with the reader, for when the poet has found an objective correlative, his job is finished.

Rhythm

The concern for structure explains Eliot's profound interest in the concept of rhythm, not only as it occurs in music, but also in verse drama and, more generally, in literary presentations. Rhythm is dependent on words and can therefore be considered an extension of the idea of the objective correlative. Eliot praised the opening scene in *Hamlet* for its verse rhythm: the lines are transparent so that

> you are consciously attending not to the poetry, but to the meaning of the poetry. The rhythm appears not only in the individual lines, but also in the dialogic exchanges.[46]

In his own works written for the stage, Eliot strove to revive the poetic drama, which was, to him, the only form of drama that was acceptable and had a chance of survival in the modern world.

Questions

Even though Eliot refers directly to the principle of the objective correlative only once, it is far from being an idiosyncratic caprice with him. It falls neatly into line with prevalent thinking in contemporary literary and critical circles, and it is a considered presentation of a significant ramification of the Zeitgeist. Hugh Kenner goes so far as to say that the idea (sc. of the objective correlative)

> makes perhaps a more general claim than Eliot intended; he could hardly have foreseen its misapplication to the job of the lyric poet.[47]

It is true that Eliot nowhere tries to apply his theory to lyrical poetry, but, as testified by the examples given earlier, it is possible to think of correlatives also in lyrical poetry. However, Eliot's categorical pronouncements raise some questions concerning the implications and consequences of the dictum. For one thing, Eliot excludes from poetic treatment the numerous situations where the stimulus comes from within the poet himself, e.g. introspective poetry. And he does not tell us what type of scenes, etc. are suitable or not suitable for his purpose. An instinctive assessment would indicate that some situations are more appropriate in poetry than others. Moreover, the use of metaphor is ignored, and a consistent application of the theory would rule out the acknowledgement of poetic diction. Elsewhere in his essays, Eliot takes up an ambivalent attitude to poetic diction. In *On Poets and Poetry* he says that the term poetic diction usually refers to obsolete words and idioms, or perhaps to words and idioms that are inappropriate in poetry. That is a remarkable assertion, and Eliot goes on to acknowledge the right of each age to have its "justified" poetic diction, which, in Eliot's perception, is neither identical with nor too distant from "current speech".[48] Thus he twists the conventional meaning of the concept of poetic diction.

The scope of correlatives is huge: an emotion like love, for example, has innumerable potentialities of illustration. The question then arises: in the case of many options, are they all equal, and, if not, who is going to decide which is the best, and what criteria for assessment can be considered valid? If the reader's reaction is not identical with the poet's, does that mean that he has misunderstood something, or that he does not benefit adequately from the reading experience? Ultimately, what is at stake, is poetic quality.

Finally, it is Eliot's contention that showing is more efficient than telling. However, showing in his case can *also* be brought about by linguistic means. A chain of events or a situation is preferable to a single word. So, poetry does have a narrative ingredient. But is the meaning of 'objective' generally agreed upon by mankind at large? Eliot would probably answer that the responsibility rests with the reader.

CONCLUSION

Eliot's critical essays often take the form of idiosyncratic but informative causeries interspersed with thought-provoking digressions. He tends to leave the subject that the title of the essay promises "in the air", and he has many personal axes to grind. He propounds a seemingly irrelevant digression, scrutinizes it, presenting it in a polemical form; sometimes he ridicules it, sometimes he rejects it, and sometimes he just proceeds to talk about what he had originally set out to do.

Eliot's theoretical reflections on what poetry 'is' or 'should be' occur as occasional remarks in his many essays. In the Preface to *The Sacred Wood* (the 1928 edition) he says that "poetry is excellent words in excellent succession",[1] and in *The Use of Poetry and the Use of Criticism* he states categorically that criticism will never arrive at a definition of poetry, or an ultimate assessment of poetry.[2] He indulges in circular reasoning: we learn what poetry is by reading good poems;[3] by the same token he says that you can learn what criticism is by reading good criticism.[4] He never wrote an *ars poetica*, and he never claimed to be the originator of a body of systematic literary doctrines or criteria. His views were too idiosyncratic to be fitted into any straitjacket.

That is not tantamount to saying that he did not take his function as critic seriously. As matter of fact, Eliot's attitude to, and treatment of, matters literary are integral parts of a larger, suggested, but never finally elaborated, social and moral edifice. Eliot almost exclusively devoted his critical acumen to poetry with drama as a close runner-up. Novels are only sporadically referred to. Sometimes he uses the word 'poetry' in the sense of literature in general; he seems to have felt that what applies to poetry, applies, *mutatis mutandis*, to other genres as well.

It is evident that to him poetry is the basic 'kind' because it illustrates and exemplifies the genuine potentialities and values of all literature. He considers drama a permanent form of art because it is able to convey greater variation, and to depict more different social types, than any other form of art.[5] No novelist worth his salt would subscribe to that statement, but the focal point of Eliot's criticism was not the novel.

And even within his two preferred genres, Eliot imposes some restrictions. He was intrigued by the concept of rhythm, so in his dealings with poetry, the emphasis is on the impact of the individual word, the concrete image, and the total rhythmical effect produced, rather than on a plot-like development as seen in epic poetry, or the lesson to be drawn from didactic poetry. To him, form goes before content. By the same token, it is a special type of drama that is admitted to the fold, viz. verse drama. There are "legitimate" demands that can only be satisfied by a drama written in verse.[6] Eliot does not elaborate the legitimacy idea, but he insists that there is a "need" among audiences for verse drama.[7] Another instance of his sometimes diffuse postulates.

"The musical phrase" is eulogized on several occasions, and it is not difficult to see a connection between the two genres favoured by Eliot. He devotes many pages to analyses of the Elizabethan dramatists' handling of blank verse, and in 20th century drama he advocates a type of prose that approaches the characteristics of the spoken language. Several of his plays are written in something reminiscent of versified prose. He admits that he finds the heroic couplet and blank verse equally unsuitable for his own purposes, but he quotes with approval numerous examples of impressive lines from Elizabethan dramatists' use of blank verse.

To him, rhythm is a scheme of organization of the way things cohere: thought, feeling and choice of words demonstrate an impeccable coalescence. What Eliot concentrates on in his dramatic analyses is the rhythmical effect of the individual speech as well as of the totality of a scene, e.g., the opening scene of *Hamlet*. The *hamartia* and the *dénouement* of a play are of decidedly peripheral significance. Social and psychological themes he finds largely irrelevant.

In his theory about the objective correlative, Eliot became an 'honest broker' between the 'out there' and the 'in here'. The existence of reality as our common sense perceives it is not questioned. The theory says nothing about the quality of the items selected as projections ("an object . . . "). The poet is the privileged seer who can visualize a similarity and thus release the poetical potential of what to other people is just "an object". In the poet's treatment, the intension of the words undergoes a change. An intimate type of interplay is thus brought about between a member of the favoured few and reality. Poets create a world of their own, based on, but different from, 'our real world', in the sense that they see parallels that remain hidden to the common man. What is to the latter just "a scene . . . " becomes to the poet an analogue of his individual response to a stimulus. Poets become a medium of interpretation of reality and impose their own vision on it. The postulate about the objective theory boils down to more than just a commonplace observation about the advantage of using 'the right word in the right place'.

Eliot implicitly agreed with the Neo-Classicists that what is ideal is best illustrated by something outside the observer. It can be justifiably argued that the Neo-Classicists' indefatigable endeavour to imitate Horace and Homer was *their* attempt at finding an objective correlative. However, what the Neo-Classicists used as their basis of comparison was not items from the phenomenal world but rather the style and themes of a select group of authors from Antiquity, who were supposed to have set covetable standards of excellence. When Neo-Classicists treated of 'our real world', as is the case in for example landscape poems, they saw the scene as an allegory. Unlike the Neo-Classicists, Eliot does not want to improve or 'heighten' the phenomena of the outside world. He took them at face value, so to speak.

And symbols do not suffice: Eliot criticizes Ben Jonson's comedies of humour for the way they depict human characters: superficially, they are human, but in reality they are nothing but a primitive instinct emerging from below the level of consciousness. They are deprived of many of the characteristics that might have provided them with a recognizable personality. Eliot's point is that they symbolize, rather than express, the given feature.[8]

Eliot was critical of the contemporary English poets who were popular with many readers. In his opinion, William Watson, Alfred Noyes and Henry Newbolt represented the nadir of English poetry. Poets and critics writing in the first decade of the 20th century had to look to France for inspiration. Eliot was fluent in French, and the diligent translations of F.S. Flint helped to familiarize his contemporaries with the novel approaches that were beginning to become perceptible across the Channel. Eliot acknowledged his debt to T.E. Hulme, who was a comrade in spirit — a classicist, a reactionary, and a fervent Christian.

French critics like Gautier, Ribot and Gourmont were instrumental in fragmenting the Positivist world picture. A central element in the rupture was an increasing focus on form rather than content. In 1912, Gustave Kahn published a seminal book on free verse (*Le vers libre*), and the French poet Jules Laforgue, whom Eliot came to know thanks to Arthur Symons' book *The Symbolist Movement in Literature*, became one of Eliot's poetical mentors owing to his linguistic inventiveness.

Gautier talked about "un tout indissociable" between the thought and the expression, i.e. the expression should be perfectly adequate to what Gautier called "l'idée".[9] Like Eliot, Gautier tended to push the reader into the background, and to both critics, the imagination became virtually synonymous with a storehouse of linguistic detail. Gourmont advocated ideas that form the germ of the dissociation of sensibility postulate. In *The Use of Poetry and the Use of Criticism*, Eliot echoed one of Gourmont's favourite theo-

ries: the intellectual element should go hand in hand with the orig-
inal intensity of feeling,[10] for poetry is worth reflection.[11] The link
to the objective correlative idea is obvious.

Both Valéry and Mallarmé stated that poetic intensity is most
surely achieved and sentimentality most surely avoided

> by using no word that directly describes a feeling or proceeds
> directly from an affective state.[12]

Poe, whose works Eliot did not admire, was known for choosing
with mathematical accuracy just the effect and just the word which
would create a perfect intimation of the supernatural in a story.[13]
Poe also thought that a poem should have nothing in view but
itself, and as his theory of the objective correlative shows, Eliot
agreed. His grievance against the Romanticists was that they used
poetry as a substitute for religion ('the poet is the priest'),[14] and his
life-long love/hate attitude to Matthew Arnold originated in the
latter's bland conception of poetry as 'a criticism of life', a state-
ment that became almost an obsession and a pet aversion with
Eliot.

Eliot cherished a warm friendship with Middleton Murry, who
said in *The Problem of Style* (whose title is a verbatim translation of
Gourmont's *Le Problème du Style*),

> style is the quality of language which communicates precisely
> emotions or thoughts, or a system of emotions or thoughts pecu-
> liar to the author.[15]

So, the concern for language and the use and function of the
individual word was a significant component of the critical
thinking of Eliot's contemporaries, and it is a safe conclusion that
the statement which is the inspiration for these pages is more than
a formulation that just occurs to him. In his opinion, poetry was
more than "merely a decoration, an added embellishment", as he
says in his defence of verse drama.[16]

Also as far as the concept of tradition is concerned Eliot stood on the shoulders of his predecessors. Writing about *The Presuppositions of Critical History* (1874), Bradley explained:

> Every man's present standpoint ought to determine his belief to *all* past events . . . History stands not only for the past in fact, but also for the present in record, and it implies in itself the union of these two elements . . . (History stands) not only for the past in fact, but also for the present in record; and it implies itself the union of these two elements.[17]

By way of a parenthetical digression, it may seem paradoxical that an age that glorified movement and dynamism (cf. Bergson's dubious, but acclaimed, postulate about *l'élan vital*) should find satisfaction in a theory which, at least in Eliot's interpretation, was, to all intents and purposes, based on stability and permanence. However, since, to Eliot, language "in its healthy state" not only presents the object, but gets so close to the object that the two are identified, it is unimaginable for a word to change its sense. Only in an uncultured philosophy do words tend to undergo changes of meaning.

Eliot's theory of the objective correlative can be seen as an argument for his instinctive dislike of *Hamlet*; perhaps he felt that some kind of critical basis would be appropriate, and perhaps he made amends to Shakespeare by using an example from another of the bard's plays to illustrate what he was getting at.

He touches on the idea — without using the term — sporadically in his oeuvre: in the essay *What is a Classic* from 1914, he discusses the *Aeneid*, saying that Aeneas' meeting with Dido is one of the most moving passages in all literature — complex in meaning and economical in expression. The scene conveys an impression of Aeneas' mood as well as of Dido's. Dido's behaviour is virtually a projection of Aeneas' own consciousness.[18] In the same essay he acknowledges Tennyson and Browning as poets who think; but they do not feel their thought as intimately and spontaneously as the scent of a rose.[19] And the Metaphysical Poets' forte is their search for a verbal equivalent for their states of feeling and consciousness.[20]

Eliot is rooted in the Positivist paradigm: the great challenge is understanding reality by describing it and thus mastering it. *Physis* in the Greek sense of the word is his field of interest, he acknowledges the primacy of sight among the senses, he does not assess or beautify the object of his analyses; the ideal is objectivity, and the criterion is veracity. The aim is precise rendering, and sense impressions have an immediate truth value. He agrees with Gourmont that man is born with a need for truth, and beauty — a word rarely used by Eliot — is achieved when the criterion of truth is fulfilled.

The poet depends for his inspiration on stimuli from 'our real world', and when the processing by the poet's intellect has been accomplished, the yardstick of success is again provided by items from outside the poet. That is a far cry from Montaigne's famous statement "Je suis moi-mesme le sujet de mon livre". In Eliot's theory, an intimate cooperation is established between the poet and reality. Reality has to be processed by a human mind in order to be properly appreciated. It is of crucial importance to realize that, to Eliot, the objective correlative is not necessarily a word. Even more, the point about it is not verbalization. As he sees it, it is a matter of "la situation juste" rather than "le mot juste". In "a set of objects . . . " etc., the linguistic aspect will normally not be the first feature that comes into a receiver's mind. It is Eliot's implied contention that "a set of objects . . . " can give the receiver an experience comparable to, but more precise than, the poet's own immediate sensory input, which, incidentally, is not formulated in words. His formulation, "a chain of events . . . " allows us to conclude that a narrative and descriptive component in poetry is admissible — even though, for his purposes, the prime concern of that component is not to narrate or describe, but to contribute to determining an emotion.

Eliot's originality resides in the fact that he states categorically that a poet has to seek the support of something outside him to find a suitable formula for his emotions. Somehow, items of reality are better qualified than words to meet Eliot's demands. Poets' usual escape route when it comes to pinpointing emotions has always been metaphorical language. Eliot agrees with many of his predecessors that if emotions are to be expressed, the best way to do it is to use figurative language. But whereas conventional metaphors — usually one or a few words — only serve to illuminate a given emotion, and have, accordingly, no 'independent' existence, Eliot's correlative is something that exists in its own right. Lady Macbeth's sleepwalking scene can be enjoyed without being perceived in terms of an objective correlative. He does not question French critics' assertion that everything can be expressed, but he circumvents it by invoking phenomena that are pre-linguistic, implying that showing is more efficient than telling.

One meaning of 'objective' as defined by OED is

> the object of perception or thought as distinct from the perceiving or thinking subject.

But if 'objective' is defined as something separate from, or opposite to, the 'subjective', the inference is that 'objective' is non-linguistic. So, Eliot does not talk of a one-to-one correspondence between an emotion and a word. Emotions are complex and are not, he thinks, adequately represented by dictionary definitions, or even by conventional metaphorical techniques The paradox is that his own poems do not live up to his ideal demand, witness the numerous, often conflicting, interpretations of them.

Eliot's theory of depersonalization fits in nicely with Positivist rules: the exclusion of the poet's personality causes poetry to approach the condition of science.[21] "No artist produces great art by endeavouring to express his own personality", he wrote in *Four Elizabethan Dramatists*.[22]

Aldington expatiates on the same idea:

We convey an emotion by presenting the object and circum-
stances of that emotion, without comment. For example we do
not say 'Oh, how I admire that beautiful, that exquisite, that –
24 more adjectives — woman', or 'O exquisite, O beautiful, O
25 more adjectives, let us spoon you for ever', but we present
that woman, we make an Image of her, we make the scene con-
vey that emotion . . . A hardness of cut stone. No slop, no
sentimentality.[23]

That statement reads like a declaration of content of Eliot's
theory.

There may be hints of the objective correlative idea in Eliot's
interest in the relationship between poetry and the social condi-
tions in which it is written. In *The Use of Poetry and the Use of
Criticism* he dwells on the fact that poetry is influenced by "the
circumstances of life":[24] changes in the function of poetry are
matched by parallel trends in society.[25] Radical changes within
poetry are signs of deeper transformations in society, and vice
versa. For example, it is his contention that Wordsworth's social
commitment inspired him to try his hand at a novel poetic form.
In the same way he saw criticism as a continuous interplay of
literary theory and prevalent social conditions. What absorbs him
in his own dramatic criticism is the *rapport* between the play and
the social context in which it came into existence, and in which it
was performed.[26] Hence his emphasis on the playwright's duties
and function and his responsibilities towards the audience. He
rejected the idea of art for art's sake for the very reason that its
adherents disclaimed any social obligation.

The socially tinted task facing poetry and criticism is very
briefly referred to in *The Use of Poetry and the Use of Criticism*, but
in actual fact very little information is given about the use of either
of the two terms on the title page. All that we are told is that it is
incumbent on poetry and criticism to be socially responsible and
have "as civilizing influence" in times of confusion.[27] However,
since *The Use of Poetry and the Use of Criticism* was written in the

early '30s, the 'confusion' would have been obvious to many readers.

As a matter of fact it does not become clear exactly what is the use of poetry if its changes are brought about by external factors. On top of this, Eliot distances himself from sociological criticism, and he abhors Shelley's idea of poets as 'the unacknowledged legislators of mankind'.

The reader plays an unobtrusive part in the theory, but his existence is taken for granted. What matters is the poet's craft and his loyalty to his own reaction. Once the poem has been composed — and Eliot agrees with Poe that writing a poem should be as conscious and deliberate as possible[28] — the poet's job is over and done with. Eliot did not write with a reader or a particular group of readers in mind. He just sends a poem into orbit, so to speak.

The concept of *le mot juste* is an ancient *topos*: Dante advised budding poets to depict "an emotion evident in the situation",[29] and Dryden and his contemporaries saw it as the task of 'elocution' to 'dress the thought'. Analysis of, and emphasis on, the use and function of the word has been continued by the New Critics and the Deconstructionists. Eliot gave the *topos* a personal twist and lifted it out of the commonplace abyss into which it has sometimes sunk. He wanted to make the verbalization process a conscious and rational pursuit, and to demonstrate that 'expressive' does not have to be synonymous with 'sentimental'. He was concerned to prove that a description found in poetry can have the same truth value as a theorem in science. Subjectivity and objectivity are a complementary pair.

Eliot said about Ben Jonson,

> He not unnaturally laid down in abstract theory what is in reality
> a personal point of view.[30]

The boomerang effect of that statement is obvious, but does not impair the relevance of Eliot's idiosyncratic treatment of a seeming commonplace.

Conclusion 59

It is only fair that the final words should be Eliot's description
of his own style in *Four Quartets*:

> where every word is at home
> Taking its place to support the others,
> The word neither diffident nor ostentatious
> An easy commerce of the old and new
> The common word exact without vulgarity
> The formal word precise but not pedantic,
> The complete consort dancing together.

NOTES

Introduction

1 Hugh Kenner, *The Invisible Poet: T.S. Eliot*, Preface, p. 9.
2 Ibid., p. 51.

CHAPTER ONE
SOME CLASSICAL PREDECESSORS

1 T.A. Moxon (ed.), *Aristotle's Poetics, Demetrius on Style, and other Classical Writings on Criticism*, p. 5.
2 Ibid.
3 *Aristotle's Poetics*, p. 51.
4 Ibid., p. 8.
5 Ibid., p. 9.
6 Ibid., p. 6.
7 Ibid.
8 Ibid.
9 Ibid., p. 39.
10 Ibid., p. 43.
11 Ibid., p. 15.
12 Ibid., p. 43.
13 Ibid., p. 9.
14 Ibid., p. 213.
15 Ibid., p. 62.
16 Ibid., p. 63.
17 Ibid., p. 71.
18 Ibid.

CHAPTER TWO
SPRAT, LOCKE, HARTMANN

1 Hugh Kenner, *The Invisible Poet*, p. 44.

2 John Locke, *An Essay Concerning Human Understanding*, Part I B, p. 25.

CHAPTER THREE
GAUTIER, BAUDELAIRE, GOURMONT

1 M.C. Spencer, *The Art Criticism of Théophile Gautier*, p. 2.
2 Ibid., p. 25.
3 Ibid., p. 127.
4 Philippe Terrier (ed.), *Charles Baudelaire: Théophile Gautier. Deux Etudes*, p. 246: Le dessein de traiter sous forme restreinte de petits sujets . . . Chaque pièce devait être un médaillon . . . L'auteur n'employa que les vers de huit pieds, qu'il refondit, polit et cisela avec tout le soin dont il était capable.
5 Ibid., p. 180: Il n'y a pas d'idées inexprimables.
6 Terrier, p. 210: Celui qu'une pensée, fût-ce la plus complexe, une vision la plus apocalyptique, surprend sans mots pour les réaliser, n'est pas un écrivain.
7 Ibid., p. 11.
8 Ibid., p. 17: Quand M. Delacroix compose un tableau, il regarde en lui-même au lieu de mettre le nez à la fenêtre.
9 Spencer, *The Art Criticism of Théophile Gautier*, p. 41: Tout homme qui n'a pas un monde intérieur à traduire n'est pas un artiste. L'imitation est le moyen et non le but. De tout ceci, il ne faut pas conclure que l'artiste soit purement objectif ; il est aussi objectif ; il donne et il reçoit. Il rend à la nature des signes dont il a besoin pour l'exprimer. Ces signes, il les transforme, il y ajoute, et il en ôte, selon le genre de sa pensée . . . Le peintre porte le tableau en lui-même, et, entre la nature et lui, la toile sert d'intermédiaire.
10 Terrier (ed.), *Charles Baudelaire*, p. 145.
11 Ibid., p. 43.
12 Ibid., p. 106.
13 Ibid.: La mélodie sort de sa bouche comme une vapeur sonore.
14 Ibid., p. 180.
15 Ibid., p. 13.
16 Glenn S. Burne, *Remy de Gourmont: His Ideas and Influence in England and America*, Preface, p. v.
17 Ibid., p. 19.

18 Ibid., 35.

19 Ibid., p. 21.

20 Remy de Gourmont, *Le Problème du Style*, p. 47: Qui dit style, dit mémoire visuelle et faculté métaphorique, combinées en proportions variables avec la mémoire émotive et tout l'apport obscur des autres sens.

21 Ibid., p. 98.

22 Ibid.

23 Ibid., p. 64: Les sens sont la porte unique par où est entré tout ce qui vit dans l'esprit . . . Une idée n'est qu'une sensation défraîchie, une image effacée.

24 Burne, *Remy de Gourmont*, p. 46.

25 Remy de Gourmont, *Le Problème du Style*, 35: La mémoire visuelle, ce réservoir d'images où puise l'imagination pour de nouvelles et infinies combinaisons.

26 Ibid., p. 44: Enfin il est constant qu'il y a des hommes en qui tout mot suscite une vision et qui n'ont jamais rédigé la plus imaginaire description sans en avoir le modèle exact sous leur regard intérieur.

27 Ibid., p. 73: Les sens se développent par cette éducation naturelle que donne la vie . . . C'est la vie, c'est l'habitude des sensations qui créera l'image stylistique.

28 T.S. Eliot, *The Sacred Wood*, pp. 14–15.

29 Burne, *Remy de Gourmont*, p. 44.

30 Eliot, *The The Sacred Wood*, pp. 56–58.

31 Remy de Gourmont, *Le Problème du Style*, p. 35: Si, à la mémoire visuelle, l'écrivain joint la mémoire émotive, s'il a le pouvoir, en évoquant un spectacle matériel, de se replacer exactement dans l'état émotionel que suscita en lui ce spectacle, il possède, même ignorant, tout l'art d'écrire.

32 Ibid., p. 151: En littérature, le fond des choses a une importance absolue . . . Rien ne meurt plus vite que le style qui ne s'appuie pas sur la solidité d'une forte pensée.

33 Ibid., p. 70: La logique de l'œil et la logique de chacun des autres sens suffisent à guider l'esprit.

34 Ibid., p. 39: Les mots n'ont de sens que par le sentiment qu'ils renferment et dont on leur confère la représentation . . . Les mots les plus inertes peuvent devenir sentiments . . . Tout mot, toute locution, les

proverbes même, les clichés vont devenir pour l'écrivain émotif des
noyaux de cristallisation sentimentale.

35 Burne, *Remy de Gourmont*, p. 101.
36 Ibid., p. 64.
37 T.S. Eliot, 'The Metaphysical Poets' in *Selected Essays.*
38 T.S. Eliot, *Selected Essays 1917–32*, p. 249.
39 Burne, *Remy de Gourmont*, p. 134.
40 Ibid., p. 80.
41 Eliot, *The Sacred Wood*, pp. 8–12.
42 Burne, *Remy de Gourmont*, p. 147.

CHAPTER FOUR
POSITIVISM AND SOME REACTIONS AGAINST IT

1 Flemming Olsen, *Between Positivism and T.S. Eliot: Imagism and T.E. Hulme*, p. 33.
2 Ibid., p. 41.
3 Ibid., p. 29.
4 Ibid., p. 43.
5 *Appearance and Reality*, p. 310.
6 Guy Stock, 'Bradley's Theory of Judgement' in Anthony Stock Manser and Guy Stock (eds.), *The Philosophy of Francis Herbert Bradley*, p. 132.
7 Georg Wilhem Frederick Hegel, *Wissenschaft der Logik*, vol. 5, p. 20.
8 Anthony Stock Manser and Guy Stock (eds.), *The Philosophy of Francis Herbert Bradley*, p. 27.
9 Hugh Kenner, *The Invisible Poet: T.S. Eliot*, p. 8.

CHAPTER FIVE
THE OBJECTIVE CORRELATIVE

1 T.S. Eliot, *The Sacred Wood* (1969 ed.), pp. 100–102. Eliot's italics.
2 Jon Margolis, *T.S. Eliot's Intellectual Development*, p. 99.
3 T.S. Eliot, *Selected Essays*, p. 145.
4 Hugh Kenner, *The Invisible Poet: T.S Eliot*, p. 291.
5 Ibid., p. 20.
6 Kenner, p. 48.
7 *On Poetry and Poets*, p. 20.
8 Ibid., p. 65.

9 Ibid., p. 69.
10 Ibid., p. 85.
11 Eliot, *Selected Essays*, p. 17.
12 Ibid., p. 20.
13 William Skaff, *The Philosophy of T.S. Eliot*, p. 93.
14 Kenner, *The Invisible Poet*, p. 103.
15 Ibid., p. 103.
16 Eliot, *Selected Essays*, p. 114.
17 Ibid., p. 145.
18 Ibid., pp. 147 et seq.
19 The essay was written in 1926 and published in the collection of essays *For Lancelot Andrewes* in 1928; pp. 28–30.
20 Francis Herbert Bradley, *Collected Essays*, p. 67.
21 Ibid., p. 9.
22 Ibid., p. 112.
23 Eliot, *Selected Essays*, p. 21.
24 Middleton Murry, *The Problem of Style*, p. 67.
25 Eliot, *The Sacred Wood* (1928), p. 168.
26 Eliot, *Selected Essays*, p. 236.
27 Francis Herbert Bradley, *Collected Essays*, p. 208.
28 Eliot, *Selected Essays*, p. 21.
29 T. S. Eliot, 'Association and Thought', *Collected Essays*, p. 216.
30 Murry, *The Problem of Style*, p. 21.
31 Skaff, *The Philosophy of T.S. Eliot*, p. 68.
32 C.K. Stead, *The New Poetic: Yeats to Eliot*, p. 136.
33 Eliot, *Selected Essays,* p. 68.
34 Ibid.
35 Kenner, *The Invisible Poet*, p. 54.
36 Cf. Flemming Olsen, *Between Positivism and T.S. Eliot: Imagism and T.E. Hulme.*
37 Ibid., p. 115.
38 Skaff, *The Philosophy of T.S. Eliot*, p. 154.
39 Flemming Olsen, *Ernest Fenollosa: 'The Chinese Written Character as a Medium for Poetry': Ars Poetica or the Roots of Poetic Creation?*
41 Skaff, *The Philosophy of T.S. Eliot*, p. 48.
42 T.S. Eliot, *The Use of Poetry and the Use of Criticism*, pp. 18–19.
43 Ibid., p. 151.

44 Ibid., p. 24.

45 T.S. Eliot, *Poetry and Drama*, pp. 15 et seq.

46 Ibid., p. 16.

47 Kenner, *The Invisible Poet: T.S. Eliot*, p. 88.

48 Ibid., p.185.

Conclusion

1 T.S. Eliot, *The Sacred Wood*, p. iv.

2 Ibid., p. 16.

3 Ibid.

4 T.S. Eliot, *The Use of Poetry and the Use of Criticism*, p. 20.

5 *The Sacred Wood* (1969), p. 61.

6 'The Possibilities of a Poetic Drama', *The Sacred Wood* (1969), p. 61.

7 Ibid.

8 William Skaff, *The Philosophy of T.S. Eliot*, p. 97.

9 Philippe Terrier (ed.), *Charles Baudelaire: Théophile Gautier. Deux Etudes*, p. 149.

10 Ibid., p. 19.

11 Ibid., p. 18.

12 Norman Suckling, *Paul Valéry and the Civilized Mind*, p. 81.

13 Robert Regan (ed.), *Poe: A Collection of Critical Essays*, p. 52.

14 T.S. Eliot, *The Use of Poetry and the Use of Criticism*, p. 26.

15 Middleton Murry, *The Problem of Style*, p. 65.

16 T.S. Eliot, *Poetry and Drama*, p. 10.

17 Francis Herbert Bradley, *Collected Essays*, pp. 2–8.

18 T.S. Eliot, *On Poetry and Poets*, p. 62.

19 Ibid., p. 65.

20 T.S. Eliot, 'The Metaphysical Poets' in *Selected Essays* (1932), p. 289.

21 'Tradition and the Individual Talent' in *The Sacred Wood* (1969), pp. 52–53.

22 Eliot, *Selected Essays* (1932), p. 114.

23 'Modern Poetry and the Imagists', *The Egoist*, 1st March 1915.

24 p. 20.

25 p. 23.

26 Eliot, *The Use of Poetry and the Use of Criticism*, p. 27.

27 Ibid., pp. 14–15.

28 Regan, *Poe: A Collection of Critical Essays*, p. 174.

29 C.K. Stead, *The New Poetic*, p. 127.
30 Eliot, *Selected Essays*, p. 156.

BIBLIOGRAPHY

Aldington, Richard, 'Modern Poetry and the Imagists'. The Egoist, 1st March 1915.

Berger, John, Ways of Seeing. A Pelican Original, 1976.

Bornstein, George, Transformation and Romanticism in Yeats, Eliot and Stevens. University of Chicago Press, 1976.

Bradley, Francis Herbert, Appearance and Reality. Oxford, 1897.

——, Essays on Truth and Reality. Oxford, 1914.

——, The Principles of Logic. Corrected Impression Oxford, 1928.

——, Collected Essays, vols 1 & 2. Oxford, Clarendon, 1935.

Bryce, A. Hamilton (ed.), The Poems of Horace. A Literal Translation. Bell & Sons, London, 1902.

Burne, Glenn S., Remy de Gourmont: His Ideas and Influence in England and America. Southern Illinois University Press, 1963.

Clarke, Graham, T.S. Eliot, Critical Assessments. London, Christopher Helm, 1990.

Davidson, Harriet, T.S. Eliot. Longman, 1999.

Debauve, J.L., Laforgue en son temps. Edition de la Baconnière. Neuchâtel Langages. Documents, 1972.

Dottin, Mireille (ed.), Jules Laforgue. Textes de critique d'art. Presses Universitaires de Lille, 1972.

Eliot, T.S., For Lancelot Andrewes. Essays on Style and Order. London, Faber & Gwyer, 1928.

——, Selected Essays. London, Faber & Faber, 1932.

——, After Strange Gods. New York, Harcourt, Brace & Co, 1933.

——, The Use of Poetry and the Use of Criticism. London, Faber & Faber, 1933.

——, Poetry and Drama. Harvard University Press, 1951.

——, The Three Voices of Poetry. Cambridge, National Book League, 1955.

——, *On Poetry and Poets*. Fifth Impression. London, Faber & Faber, 1960.

——, *Knowledge and Experience in the Philosophy of F.H.Bradley*. Faber & Faber, 1964.

——, *To Criticize the Critic*. New York, Farrar, Straus & Giroux, 1965.

——, *The Sacred Wood*. 1960, repr. 1969. Methuen, London.

Fabricius, Johannes, *The Unconscious and Mr. Eliot*. Copenhagen, 1967.

Fauconnier, G. & Turner, M., *The Way We Think*. New York, 2002.

Gardner, Helen, *The Art of T.S. Eliot*. Cresset Press, 1949, re-issue 1968.

Gautier, Théophile, *Emaux et Camées*. Paris, 1852.

——, *L'Art*. Paris, 1857.

Gourmont, Remy de, *Le Livre des Masques*. Sixième éd., Paris, Mercure de France, 1896.

——, *Promenades littéraires*. 1ᵉ série 1904, 2me série 1906, 3me série 1909, 4me série 1912, 5me série 1913. Paris, Mercure de France.

——, *La Culture des Idées*. Paris, 1900.

——, *Le Problème du Style*. Paris, 1924.

Grant, Michael, *T.S. Eliot. The Critical Heritage*. London, 1982.

Hartmann, Eduard von, *Philosophy of the Unconscious*. Transl. from German *Philosophie des Unbewussten* by William Chatterton Coupland. London, Kegan Paul, Trench, Trubner & Co. Ltd, 1931.

Hjelmslev, Louis, *Prolegomena to a Theory of Language* (1949): transl. Francis Whitfield. Madison, University of Wisconsin Press,1961.

Kenner, Hugh, *The Invisible Poet: T.S. Eliot*. London, Methuen, University Paperback, Repr. 1979.

Kojecky, Roger, *T.S. Eliot's Social Criticism*. New York, 1972.

Locke, John, *An Essay Concerning Human Understanding*. London, 1690.

Manser, Anthony Stock & Stock, Guy (eds.), *The Philosophy of Francis Herbert Bradley*. Oxford, Clarendon, 1986.

Margolis, John D., *T.S. Eliot's Intellectual Development 1922–1939*. University of Chicago Press, 1972.

Martin, C.G. (ed.), *Eliot in Perspective: a Symposium*. Macmillan, 1970.

Matthiessen, F.O., *The Achievement of T.S. Eliot*. Oxford University Press, 1947.

Moody, A. David, *The Cambridge Companion to T.S. Eliot*. Cambridge University Press, 1998.

Moxon, T.A. (ed.), *Aristotle's Poetics. Demetrius on Style. And Other Classical*

Writings on Criticism. London, Everyman's Library 901, 1943.

Murry, John Middleton, *The Problem of Style.* Sixth Impr., Oxford University Press, 1975.

Newton-De Molina, *The Literary Criticism of T.S. Eliot: NewEssays.* London, 1972.

Olsen, Flemming, *Between Positivism and T.S. Eliot: Imagism and T.E. Hulme.* University Press of Southern Denmark, 2008.

——, *Ernest Fenollosa 'The Chinese Written Character as a Medium for Poetry': Ars Poetica or the Roots of Poetic Creation?* Brighton, Portland, Toronto, Sussex Academic Press, 2011.

Peirce, Charles Sanders, *Reasoning and the Logic of Things.* Harvard University Press, 1992.

Regan, Robert (ed.), *Poe. A Collection of Critical Essays.* Prentice-Hall, 1967.

Ribot, Théodule, *L'Imagination créatrice.* Paris, 1900.

Sharpe, Tony, *T.S. Eliot, A Literary Life.* Basingstoke, Macmillan, 1991.

Skaff, William, *The Philosophy of T.S. Eliot: From Skepticism to a Surrealist Poetic 1909–1927.* University of Pennsylvania Press, 1986.

Spencer, Michael Clifford, *The Art Criticism of Théophile Gautier.* Genève, Librairie Droz, 1969.

Sprat, Thomas, *History of the Royal Society.* London, 1667.

Spurr, David, *Conflicts in Consciousness. T.S. Eliot's Poetry and Criticism.* University of Illinois Press, 1984.

Stead, C.K., *The New Poetic: Yeats to Eliot.* London, Hutchinson University Library, 1975.

Suckling, Norman, *Paul Valéry and the Civilized Mind.* London, 1955.

Sullivan Sheila (ed.), *Critics on T.S. Eliot: Readings in Literary Criticism.* London, Allen & Unwin, 1973.

Tate, Allen (ed.), *T.S. Eliot: The Man and His Work.* New York, Delacorte, New York, 1966.

Terrier, Philippe (ed.), *Charles Baudelaire. Théophile Gautier. Deux Etudes.* Neuchâtel, 1985.

Unger, Leonard (ed.), *T.S.Eliot: A Selected Critique.* Rinehart, New York, 1948.

Valéry, Paul, *Introduction à la Poétique.* Gallimard ,1938.

Williamson, George, *A Reader's Guide to T.S. Eliot.* Thames & Hudson 1955, 2nd ed. 1966.

INDEX

Printed and bound by CPI Group (UK) Ltd, Croydon, CR0 4YY

10/06/2025

14686697-0001